Kidney D
for Inexperienced cooks 2021

Choose tasty and healthy recipes for your kidneys: stop boredom in the kitchen

ALICIA COLLIN

The following Book is reproduced below with the goal of providing information that is as accurate and reliable as possible. Regardless, purchasing this Book can be seen as consent to the fact that both the publisher and the author of this book are in no way experts on the topics discussed within and that any recommendations or suggestions that are made herein are for entertainment purposes only. Professionals should be consulted as needed prior to undertaking any of the action endorsed herein.

This declaration is deemed fair and valid by both the American Bar Association and the Committee of Publishers Association and is legally binding throughout the United States.

The information in the following pages is broadly considered a truthful and accurate account of facts and as such, any inattention, use, or misuse of the information in question by the reader will render any resulting actions solely under their purview. There are no scenarios in which the publisher or the original author of this work can be in any fashion deemed liable for any hardship or damages that may befall them after undertaking information described herein.

Additionally, the information in the following pages is intended only for informational purposes and should thus be thought of as universal. As befitting its nature, it is presented without assurance regarding its prolonged validity or interim quality. Trademarks that are mentioned are done without written consent and can in no way be considered an endorsement from the trademark holder.

TABLE OF CONTANTS

Introduction

INTRODUCTION

Eating healthy is definitely the first step in helping our bodies cleanse and get better.If you've been diagnosed with chronic kidney disease, a kidney diet is an important part of your treatment plan. It's very important to understand what renal diets are and why they are so important to the health of your kidneys - and your overall longevity.

What is Renal Diet?

Renal diet is a special diet that is formulated for people who have chronic kidney disease (CKD). A renal diet is sometimes referred to as a "low potassium" or "low phosphorus" diet. While the actual restrictions vary, all renal diets help to reduce blood pressure and lessen strain on your kidneys.

What Does a Renal Diet Consist of?

The precise components of any given renal diet will depend upon the needs of your particular case. If you are at risk of developing kidney stones, you're likely be asked to reduce calcium as well. Rigorous case-by-case analysis is necessary, but generally a renal diet will include:

- Dairy products, including milk, cheese and yogurt
- Legumes (such as beans)
- Fruit and fruit juices
- Nuts and nut oils (such as peanut oil)
- Soy products and soy protein supplements

High salt foods (sodium chloride) or supplements (sodium chloride) to reduce your risk of kidney stones Although you may be able to eat most of these foods without suffering harmful effects, your doctor might recommend limitations: You should be very careful about how much salt you consume. Sodium bicarbonate can be added to the diet to help with absorption. You should limit potassium intake. Foods high in potassium such as bananas, apricots and avocados should be avoided. Potassium can be replaced with magnesium citrate or sodium bicarbonate. You should limit your fluid and electrolyte intake, which could increase urinary calcium excretion. Vegetarian diets include a greater variety of foods than non-vegetarian diets that are not usually limited, but strict vegetarian diets might be necessary to avoid inadequate calcium intake

How Is a Renal Diet Administered?

In general, the renal diet is served in three phases: initiation, continuation (or secondary) and maintenance. During the initiation phase you'll eat approximately 70% of total calories as protein and carbs – with 30% to 40% coming from other nutrients.

This phase lasts for approximately a month.

In continuation phase you will consume the same daily calorie total as in the initiation phase, which is about 60% protein and 40% carbs.

However, you will try to get more vegetables and fruits into your diet now. You should get 20% of your calories from fat during this phase.

When your renal function has stabilized (and not before), you have completed the maintenance phase of the renal diet. For many people with CKD, this means switching to a low-sodium diet in addition to the low potassium/low phosphorus diet.

Benefits of the Renal Diet

The reason for following a renal diet is to reduce strain on the kidneys. By keeping your phosphorus and potassium intake low, you can reduce the risk of developing renal osteodystrophy, a condition which involves changes in bone caused by high blood pressure in the kidneys.
Additionally, there's some evidence that a renal diet helps preserve kidney function by decreasing proteinuria (a urine test used to detect protein in the urine that indicates damage to the kidneys). If you continue to consume too much phosphorus and potassium and do not follow a renal diet, your doctor may recommend that you undergo dialysis treatment.
There's evidence that following a renal diet may also result in significant weight loss. While there is some debate about the effects of a renal diet on weight loss, one study found that while following a renal diet, study participants lost 9.4 pounds over 3 months without any change in their calorie intake.

Side Effects of the Renal Diet

Although the renal diet helps to keep your kidneys healthy and can reduce the risk of kidney damage, it can also lead to problems if you don't eat enough salt or if you follow an extremely strict dietary plan.
If you consume an adequate number of calories but do not allow for necessary amounts of sodium and potassium in your diet, you can end up with serious health consequences.
While the risk of developing severe side, effects is low with an adequate and well-balanced diet, you might experience nausea, vomiting, dizziness and muscle weakness.
If you stop consuming enough salt your body will try to compensate by taking it from tissue fluid. This can lead to

hypovolemia (low blood volume) and a drop in blood pressure.
If you severely restrict the amount of potassium in your diet or if you follow a strict vegetarian diet, your kidneys might actually become damaged by phosphaturia, a condition which results from consuming too much protein in relation to the amount of phosphorus in the body.
This cookbook will help you transition to a renal diet. It includes all the foods and recipes you'll need to be successful.

Breakfast

Panzanella Salad

Preparation Time: 10 minutes

Cooking Time: 5 minutes

Servings: 4

Ingredients:

- 2 cucumbers, chopped
- 1 red onion, sliced
- 2 red bell peppers, chopped
- ¼ cup fresh cilantro, chopped
- 1 tablespoon capers
- 1 oz whole-grain bread, chopped
- 1 tablespoon canola oil
- ½ teaspoon minced garlic
- 1 tablespoon Dijon mustard
- 1 teaspoon olive oil
- 1 teaspoon lime juice

Directions:

1. Pour canola oil into the skillet and bring it to boil.
2. Add chopped bread and roast it until crunchy (3-5 minutes).
3. Meanwhile, in the salad bowl, combine sliced red onion, cucumbers, bell peppers, cilantro, capers, and mix up gently.

4. Make the dressing: mix up together lime juice, olive oil, Dijon mustard, and minced garlic.
5. Put the dressing over the salad and stir it directly before serving.
6.

Nutrition: Calories: 224.3 Fat: 10g Carbs: 26g Protein: 6.6g Sodium: 401mg Potassium: 324.9mg Phosphorus: 84mg

Coconut Breakfast Smoothie

Preparation Time: 5 minutes

Cooking Time: 5 minutes

Servings: 1

Ingredients:

- 1/4 cup whey protein powder
- 1/2 cup coconut milk
- 5 drops liquid stevia
- 1 tbsp coconut oil
- 1 tsp vanilla
- 2 tbsp coconut butter
- 1/4 cup water
- 1/2 cup ice

Directions:

1. Add all ingredients into the blender and blend until smooth.
2. Serve and enjoy.

Nutrition: Calories 560 Fat 45 g Carbohydrates 12 g Sugar 4 g Protein 25 g Cholesterol 60 mg Phosphorus: 160mg Potassium: 127mg Sodium: 85mg

Blueberry Muffins

Preparation Time: 15 minutes

Cooking Time: 30 minutes

Servings: 12

Ingredients:

- 2 cups Unsweetened rice milk
- 1 Tbsp. Apple cider vinegar
- 3 ½ cups All-purpose flour
- 1 cup Granulated sugar
- 1 Tbsp. Baking soda substitute
- 1 tsp. Ground cinnamon
- ½ tsp. Ground nutmeg
- Pinch ground ginger
- ½ cup Canola oil
- 2 Tbsps. Pure vanilla extract
- 2 ½ cups Fresh blueberries

Directions:

1. Preheat the oven to 375F.
2. Prepare a muffin pan and set aside.
3. Stir together the rice milk and vinegar in a small bowl. Set aside for 10 minutes.
4. In a large bowl, stir together the sugar, flour, baking soda, cinnamon, nutmeg, and ginger until well mixed.
5. Add oil and vanilla to the milk and mix.

6. Put milk mixture to dry ingredients and stir well to combine.
7. Put the blueberries and spoon the muffin batter evenly into the cups.
8. Bake the muffins for 25 to 30 minutes or until golden and a toothpick inserted comes out clean.
9. Cool for 15 minutes and serve.

Nutrition: Calories: 331 Fat: 11g Carb: 52g Sugar 3g Protein: 6g Sodium: 35mg Potassium: 89mg Phosphorus: 90mg

Mexican Style Burritos

Preparation Time: 5 minutes

Cooking Time: 15 minutes

Servings: 2

Ingredients:

- 1 tbsp. Olive oil
- 2 Corn tortillas
- ¼ cup chopped Red onion
- ¼ cup chopped Red bell peppers
- ½, deseeded and chopped red chili
- 2 Eggs
- 1 lime juice
- 1 tbsp. chopped Cilantro

Directions:

1. Place the tortillas in medium heat for 1 to 2 minutes on each side or until lightly toasted.
2. Remove and keep the broiler on.
3. Heat the oil in a skillet and sauté onion, chili, and bell peppers for 5 to 6 minutes or until soft.
4. Crack the eggs over the top of the onions and peppers.
5. Place skillet under the broiler for 5 to 6 minutes or until the eggs are cooked.
6. Serve half the eggs and vegetables on top of each tortilla and sprinkle with cilantro and lime juice to serve.

Nutrition: Calories: 202 Fat: 13g Sugar 1g Carb: 19g Protein: 9g Sodium: 77mg Potassium: 233mg Phosphorus: 184mg

Bulgur, Couscous, And Buckwheat Cereal

Preparation Time: 10 minutes

Cooking Time: 25 minutes

Servings: 4

Ingredients:

- 2 ¼ cups Water
- 1 ¼ cups Vanilla rice milk
- 6 Tbsps. Uncooked bulgur
- 2 Tbsps. Uncooked whole buckwheat
- 1 cup Sliced apple
- 6 Tbsps. Plain uncooked couscous
- ½ tsp. Ground cinnamon

Directions:

1. Heat the water and milk in the saucepan over medium heat. Let it boil.
2. Put the bulgur, buckwheat, and apple.
3. Reduce the heat to low and simmer, occasionally stirring until the bulgur is tender, about 20 to 25 minutes.
4. Remove the saucepan and stir in the couscous and cinnamon—cover for 10 minutes.
5. Put the cereal before serving.

Nutrition: Calories: 159 Fat: 1g Carb: 34g Sugar 5g Protein: 4g Sodium: 33mg Potassium: 116m Phosphorus: 130mg

Egg And Veggie Muffins

Preparation Time: 15 minutes

Cooking Time: 20 minutes

Servings: 4

Ingredients:

- 4 Eggs
- 2 Tbsp. Unsweetened rice milk
- ½ chopped Sweet onion
- ½ chopped Red bell pepper
- Pinch red pepper flakes
- Pinch ground black pepper

Directions:

1. Preheat the oven to 350F.
2. Spray 4 muffin pans with cooking spray. Set aside.
3. Whisk the milk, eggs, onion, red pepper, parsley, red pepper flakes, and black pepper until mixed.
4. Pour the egg mixture into prepared muffin pans.
5. Bake until the muffins are puffed and golden, about 18 to 20 minutes. Serve.

Nutrition: Calories: 84 Fat: 5g Carb: 3g Protein: 7g Sodium: 75mg Potassium: 117mg Phosphorus: 110mg

Lunch

Mushrooms Velvet Soup

Preparation Time: 40 minutes

Cooking Time: 40 minutes

Servings: 6

Ingredients:

- 1 teaspoon olive oil
- ½ teaspoon fresh ground black pepper
- 3 medium (85g) shallots, diced
- 2 stalks (80g) celery, chopped
- 1 clove garlic, diced
- 12-ounces cremini mushrooms, sliced
- 5 tablespoons flour
- 4 cups low sodium vegetable stock, divided
- 3 sprigs fresh thyme
- 2 bay leaves
- ½ cup regular yogurt

Directions:

1. Heat oil in a large pan.
2. Add ground pepper, shallots and celery. Cook over medium-high heat.
3. Sauté for 2 minutes until golden.
4. Add garlic and stir.
5. Include the sliced mushrooms. Stir and cook until the mushrooms give out their liquid.

6. Sprawl the flour on the mushrooms and toast for about 2 min.
7. Add one cup of hot stock, thyme sprigs and bay leaves. Stir and add the second cup of stock
8. Stir until well combined.
9. Add the remaining cups of stock.
10. Slowly cook for 15 minutes.
11. Take out bay leaves and thyme sprigs.
12. Blend until mixture is smooth.
13. Include the yogurt and stir well.
14. Slowly cook for 4 minutes.
15. Serve and enjoy!

Nutrition: Calories 126 Fat 8 g Cholesterol 0 mg Carbohydrate 14 g Sugar 4 g Fiber 2 g Protein 3 g Sodium 108 mg Calcium 55 mg Phosphorus 70 mg Potassium 298 mg

Aromatic Carrot Cream

Preparation Time: 15 minutes

Cooking Time: 25 minutes

Servings: 4

Ingredients:

- 1 tablespoon olive oil
- ½ sweet onion, chopped
- 2 teaspoons fresh ginger, peeled and grated
- 1 teaspoon fresh garlic, minced
- 4 cups water
- 3 carrots, chopped
- 1 teaspoon ground turmeric
- ½ cup coconut almond milk

Directions:

1. Heat the olive oil into a big pan over medium-high heat.
2. Add the onion, garlic and ginger. Softly cook for about 3 minutes until softened.
3. Include the water, turmeric and the carrots. Softly cook for about 20 minutes (until the carrots are softened).
4. Blend the soup adding coconut almond milk until creamy.
5. Serve and enjoy!

Nutrition: Calories 112 Fat 10 g Cholesterol 0 mg Carbohydrates 8 g Sugar 5 g Fiber 2 g Protein 2 g Sodium 35 mg Calcium 32 mg Phosphorus 59 mg Potassium 241 mg

Lettuce Wraps With Chicken

Preparation Time: 10 minutes

Cooking Time: 15 minutes

Servings: 4

Ingredients:

- 8 lettuce leaves
- .25 cups of fresh cilantro
- .25 cups of mushroom
- 1 tsp. of five spices seasoning
- .25 cups of onion
- 6 tsp. of rice vinegar
- 2 tsp. of hoisin
- 6 tsp. of oil (canola)
- 3 tsp. of oil (sesame)
- 2 tsp. of garlic
- 2 scallions
- 8 ounces of cooked chicken breast

Directions:

1. Mince together the cooked chicken and the garlic. Chop up the onions, cilantro, mushrooms, and scallions.
2. Use a skillet overheat, combine chicken to all remaining ingredients, minus the lettuce leaves. Cook for fifteen minutes, stirring occasionally.
3. Place .25 cups of the mixture into each leaf of lettuce.
4. Wrap the lettuce around like a burrito and eat.

Nutrition: Calories: 84 Fat: 4g Carbs: 9g Protein: 5.9g Sodium: 618mg Potassium: 258mg Phosphorus: 64mg

Chicken Tacos

Preparation Time: 5 minutes

Cooking Time: 20 minutes

Servings: 4

Ingredients:

- 8 corn tortillas
- 1.5 tsp. of Sodium-free taco seasoning
- 1 juiced lime
- .5 cups of cilantro
- 2 green onions, chopped
- 8 oz. of iceberg or romaine lettuce, shredded or chopped
- .25 cup of sour cream
- 1 pound of boneless and skinless chicken breast

Directions:

1. Cook chicken, by boiling, for twenty minutes. Shred or chop cooked chicken into fine bite-sized pieces.
2. Mix the seasoning and lime juice with the chicken.
3. Put chicken mixture and lettuce in tortillas.
4. Top with the green onions, cilantro, and sour cream.

Nutrition: Calories: 260 Fat: 3g Carbs: 36g Protein: 23g Sodium: 922mg Potassium: 445mg Phosphorus: 357mg

Marinated Shrimp Pasta Salad

Preparation Time: 15 minutes

Cooking Time: 5 hours

Servings: 1

Ingredients:

- 1/4 cup of honey
- 1/4 cup of balsamic vinegar
- 1/2 of an English cucumber, cubed
- 1/2 pound of fully cooked shrimp
- 15 baby carrots
- 1.5 cups of dime-sized cut cauliflower
- 4 stalks of celery, diced
- 1/2 large yellow bell pepper (diced)
- 1/2 red onion (diced)
- 1/2 large red bell pepper (diced)
- 12 ounces of uncooked tri-color pasta (cooked)
- 3/4 cup of olive oil
- 3 tsp. of mustard (Dijon)
- 1/2 tsp. of garlic (powder)
- 1/2 tsp. pepper

Directions:

1. Cut vegetables and put them in a bowl with the shrimp.
2. Whisk together the honey, balsamic vinegar, garlic powder, pepper, and Dijon mustard in a small bowl.

While still whisking, slowly add the oil and whisk it all together.

3. Add the cooked pasta to the bowl with the shrimp and vegetables and mix it.
4. Toss the sauce to coat the pasta, shrimp, and vegetables evenly.
5. Cover and chill for a minimum of five hours before serving. Stir and serve while chilled.

Nutrition: Calories: 205 Fat: 13g Carbs: 10g Protein: 12g Sodium: 363mg Potassium: 156mg Phosphorus: 109mg

Dinner

Chicken and Apple Curry

Preparation Time: 10 minutes

Cooking Time: 1 hour and 11 minutes

Servings: 8

Ingredients:

- 8 boneless skinless chicken breasts
- 1/4 teaspoon black pepper
- 2 medium apples, peeled, cored, and chopped
- 2 small onions, chopped
- 1 garlic clove, minced
- 3 tablespoons butter
- 1 tablespoon curry powder
- 1/2 tablespoon dried basil
- 3 tablespoons flour
- 1 cup chicken broth
- 1 cup of rice almond milk

Directions:

1. Preheat oven to 350ºF.
2. Set the chicken breasts in a baking pan and sprinkle black pepper over it.
3. Place a suitably-sized saucepan over medium heat and add butter to melt.
4. Add onion, garlic, and apple, then sauté until soft.

5. Stir in basil and curry powder, and then cook for 1 minute.
6. Add flour and continue mixing for 1 minute.
7. Stir in rice almond milk and chicken broth, then stir cook for 5 minutes.
8. Pour this sauce over the chicken breasts in the baking pan.
9. Bake the chicken for 60 minutes then serve.

Nutrition: Calories: 232 kcal Total Fat: 8 g Saturated Fat: 0 g Cholesterol: 85 mg Sodium: 118 mg Total Carbs: 11 g

Very Wild Mushroom Pilaf

Preparation Time: 10 minutes

Cooking Time: 3 hours

Servings: 4

Ingredients:

- 1 cup wild rice
- 2 garlic cloves, minced
- 6 green onions, chopped
- 2 tablespoons olive oil
- ½ pound baby Bella mushrooms
- 2 cups water

Directions:

1. Add rice, garlic, onion, oil, mushrooms and water to your Slow Cooker.
2. Stir well until mixed.
3. Place lid and cook on LOW for 3 hours.
4. Stir pilaf and divide between serving platters.
5. Enjoy!

Nutrition: Calories: 210 Fat: 7g Carbohydrates: 16g Protein: 4g Phosphorus: 110mg Potassium: 117mg Sodium: 75mg

Caribbean Turkey Curry

Preparation Time: 10 minutes

Cooking Time: 1 hour a 30 minutes

Servings: 6

Ingredients:

- 3 1/2 lbs. turkey breast, with skin
- 1/4 cup butter, melted
- 1/4 cup honey
- 1 tbsp. mustard
- 2 tsp. curry powder
- 1 tsp. garlic powder

Directions:

1. Place the turkey breast in a shallow roasting pan.
2. Insert a meat thermometer to monitor the temperature.
3. Bake the turkey for 1.5 hours at 350 degrees' f until its internal temperature reaches 170 degrees f.
4. Meanwhile, thoroughly mix honey, butter, curry powder, garlic powder, and mustard in a bowl.
5. Glaze the cooked turkey with this mixture liberally.
6. Let it sit for 15 minutes for absorption.
7. Slice and serve.

Nutrition: Calories: 275 kcal Total Fat: 13 g Saturated Fat: 0 g Cholesterol: 82 mg Sodium: 122 mg Total Carbs: 90 g

Chicken Veronique

Preparation Time: 10 minutes

Cooking Time: 10 minutes

Servings: 4

Ingredients:

- 2 boneless skinless chicken breasts
- 1/2 shallot, chopped
- 2 tablespoons butter
- 2 tablespoons dry white wine
- 2 tablespoons chicken broth
- 1/2 cup green grapes, halved
- 1 teaspoon dried tarragon
- 1/4 cup cream

Directions:

1. Place an 8-inch skillet over medium heat and add butter to melt.
2. Sear the chicken in the melted butter until golden-brown on both sides.
3. Place the boneless chicken on a plate and set it aside.
4. Add shallot to the same skillet and stir until soft.
5. Whisk cornstarch with broth and wine in a small bowl.
6. Pour this slurry into the skillet and mix well.
7. Place the chicken in the skillet and cook it on a simmer for 6 minutes.
8. Transfer the chicken to the serving plate.

9. Add cream, tarragon, and grapes.
10. Cook for 1 minute, and then pour this sauce over the chicken.
11. Serve.

Nutrition: Calories: 306 kcal Total Fat: 18 g Saturated Fat: 0 g Cholesterol: 124 mg Sodium: 167 mg Total Carbs: 9 g

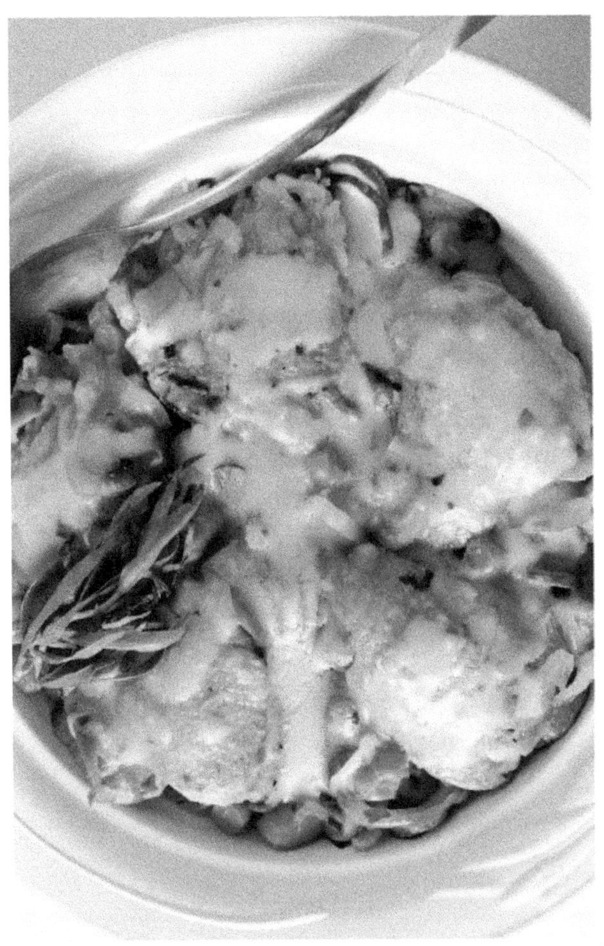

Snacks

Butternut Squash Fries

Preparation Time: 5 Minutes

Cooking Time: 10 Minutes

Servings: 2

Ingredients:

- 1 butternut squash
- 1 tbsp extra virgin olive oil
- ½ tbsp grapeseed oil
- 1/8 tsp sea salt

Directions:

1. Remove seeds from the squash and cut into thin slices. Coat with extra virgin olive oil and grapeseed oil. Add a sprinkle of salt and toss to coat well.
2. Arrange the squash slices onto three baking sheets and bake for 10 minutes until crispy.

Nutrition: calories: 40 carbs: 10g Fat: 0g Protein: 1g

Dried Fig Tapenade

Preparation Time: 5 Minutes

Cooking Time: 0 Minutes

Servings: 1

Ingredients:

- 1 cup dried figs
- 1 cup kalamata olives
- ½ cup water
- 1 tbsp chopped fresh thyme
- 1 tbsp extra virgin olive oil
- ½ tsp balsamic vinegar

Directions:

1. Prepare figs in a food processor until well chopped, add water, and continue processing to form a paste.
2. Add olives and pulse until well blended. Add thyme, vinegar, and extra virgin olive oil and pulse until very smooth. Best served with crackers of your choice.

Nutrition: calories: 249 carbs: 64g fat: 1g protein: 3g

Speedy Sweet Potato Chips

Preparation Time: 15 Minutes

Cooking Time: 0 Minutes

Servings: 4

Ingredients:

- 1 large sweet potato
- 1 tbsp extra virgin olive oil
- Salt

Directions:

1. 300°f preheated oven. Slice your potato into nice, thin slices that resemble fries.
2. Toss the potato slices with salt and extra virgin olive oil in a bowl. Bake for about one hour, flipping every 15 minutes until crispy and browned.

Nutrition: calories: 150 carbs: 16g fat: 9g protein: 1g

Nachos with Hummus (Mediterranean Inspired)

Preparation Time: 15 Minutes

Cooking Time: 20 Minutes

Servings: 4

Ingredients:

- 4 cups salted pita chips
- 1 (8 oz.) Red pepper (roasted)
- Hummus
- 1 tsp finely shredded lemon peel
- ¼ cup chopped pitted kalamata olives
- ¼ cup crumbled feta cheese
- 1 plum (roma) tomato, seeded, chopped
- ½ cup chopped cucumber
- 1 tsp chopped fresh oregano leaves

Directions:

1. 400°f preheated oven. Arrange the pita chips on a heatproof platter and drizzle with hummus.
2. Top with olives, tomato, cucumber, and cheese and bake until warmed through. Sprinkle lemon zest and oregano and enjoy while it's hot.

Nutrition:calories: 130 carbs: 18g fat: 5g protein: 4g

Stuffed Celery

Preparation Time: 15 Minutes

Cooking Time: 20 Minutes

Servings: 3

Ingredients:

- Olive oil
- 1 clove garlic, minced
- 2 tbsp pine nuts
- 2 tbsp dry-roasted sunflower seeds
- ¼ cup italian cheese blend, shredded
- 8 stalks celery leaves
- 1 (8-ounce) fat-free cream cheese
- Cooking spray

Directions:

1. Sauté garlic and pine nuts over a medium setting for the heat until the nuts are golden brown. Cut off the wide base and tops from celery.
2. Remove two thin strips from the round side of the celery to create a flat surface.
3. Mix italian cheese and cream cheese in a bowl and spread into cut celery stalks.
4. Sprinkle half of the celery pieces with sunflower seeds and a half with the pine nut mixture. Cover mixture and let stand for at least 4 hours before eating.

Nutrition: calories: 64 carbs: 2g fat: 6g protein: 1g

Hummus and Olive Pita Bread

Preparation Time: 5 Minutes

Cooking Time: 0 Minutes

Servings: 3

Ingredients:

- 7 pita bread cut into 6 wedges each
- 1 (7 ounces) container plain hummus
- 1 tbsp greek vinaigrette
- ½ cup chopped pitted kalamata olives

Directions:

1. Spread the hummus on a serving plate—mix vinaigrette and olives in a bowl and spoon over the hummus. Enjoy with wedges of pita bread.

Nutrition: calories: 225 carbs: 40g fat: 5g protein: 9g

Roast Asparagus

Preparation Time: 15 Minutes

Cooking Time: 5 Minutes

Servings: 4

Ingredients:

- 1 tbsp extra virgin olive oil (1 tablespoon)
- 1 medium lemon
- ½ tsp freshly grated nutmeg
- ½ tsp black pepper
- ½ tsp kosher salt

Directions:

1. Warm the oven to 500°f. Put the asparagus on an aluminum foil and drizzle with extra virgin olive oil, and toss until well coated.
2. Roast the asparagus in the oven for about five minutes; toss and continue roasting until browned. Sprinkle the roasted asparagus with nutmeg, salt, zest, and pepper.

Nutrition: calories: 123 carbs: 5g fat: 11g protein: 3g

Appetizers

Hummus Deviled Eggs

Preparation Time: 10 minutes

Cooking Time: 0 minutes

Servings: 6

Ingredients:

- 6 hard-boiled eggs
- 1/2 cup hummus
- Paprika

Directions:

1. Slice the hardboiled eggs in half lengthwise and remove the yolk.
2. Fill the egg whites with hummus and sprinkle with paprika before serving.

Nutrition: Calories: 179 kcal Protein: 11.03 g Fat: 12.41 g Carbohydrates: 5.14 g

Lemony Ginger Cookies

Preparation Time: 15 minutes + 30 minutes' chill time

Cooking Time: 10-12 minutes

Servings: 25

Ingredients:

- 1/2 cup arrowroot flour
- 1/2 cups stevia
- 3/4 teaspoon salt
- 1/2 teaspoon baking soda
- 1 teaspoon nutritional yeast
- inches of ginger root, peeled and diced
- 1 1/2 cup coconut butter, softened
- Zest of 1 lemon
- teaspoons vanilla

Directions:

1. Set the oven to 350F, then line two or three cookie sheets with parchment paper.
2. Mix the arrowroot flour, stevia, salt, soda, and yeast in a bowl.
3. In another bowl, put the remaining ingredients and mix well.
4. Put in the dry ingredients gradually until well combined. If the dough is too soft, put an additional 1 to 2 tablespoons of arrowroot powder. The dough will stiffen when chilled, so be careful.

5. Wrap the dough in parchment and press it flat. Chill for 30 minutes.
6. Take a chunk of the chilled dough and flatten it between two pieces of parchment until it is 1/8 inch thick. Dust with a little arrowroot powder and cut into shapes.
7. Place on baking sheets about 1 inch apart and bake 10 to 12 minutes. Cool on cookie sheets for 15 minutes before removing.

Nutrition: Calories: 112 kcal Protein: 0.44 g Fat: 11.3 g Carbohydrates: 2.49 g

Double Corn Muffins

Preparation Time: 10 minutes

Cooking Time: 20 minutes

Serving: 6

Ingredients:

- ¾ cup all-purpose flour
- ¼ cup yellow cornmeal
- 2 tablespoons brown sugar
- 1 teaspoon cream of tartar
- ½ teaspoon baking soda
- Pinch salt
- 1 large egg
- ½ cup unsweetened almond milk
- ½ cup whole kernel corn
- 3 tablespoons unsalted butter, melted

Direction

1. Preheat the oven to 350°F. Prep a 6-cup muffin pan with paper liners and set aside.
2. Scourge flour, cornmeal, brown sugar, cream of tartar, baking soda, and salt until well blended.
3. In a small bowl, stir together the egg, almond milk, corn, and melted butter.
4. Add the liquid ingredients to the dry ingredients and stir just until combined.

5. Split the batter among the prepared muffin cups, filling each about ¾ full.
6. Bake for 18 to 20 minutes or until the muffins are set and light golden brown.
7. Remove the muffins from the muffin tin and set on a wire rack to cool. Serve warm.

Nutrition: 165 Calories 160mg Sodium 55mg Phosphorus 168mg Potassium 4g Protein

Hummus with Celery

Preparation Time: 15 minutes

Cooking Time: 0 minutes

Servings: 4

Ingredients:

- 1/4 cup lemon juice
- 1/4 cup tahini
- 3 cloves of garlic, crushed
- 2 tablespoons extra virgin olive oil
- 1/2 teaspoon salt
- 1/2 teaspoon cumin
- (15–ounce) can chickpeas
- to 3 tablespoons water
- Dash of paprika
- 6 stalks celery, cut into 2-inch pieces
- tablespoons salsa

Directions:

1. Using a food processor mix the lemon juice and tahini for about a minute, until it is smooth. Scrape the sides down and process for 30 more seconds.
2. Add the garlic, olive oil, salt, and cumin. Blend for about 1 minute.
3. Drain the chickpeas, put the half of them on the food processor, and blend for another minute. Scrape down the sides, add the other half of the chickpeas, and

process until smooth, about 2 minutes. If it like a little too thick, add water, 1 tablespoon at a time until you reach the desired consistency.

4. Fill the celery sticks with hummus and sprinkle paprika on top.
5. Serve with salsa for dipping.

Nutrition: Calories: 240 kcal Protein: 9.27 g Fat: 14.51 g Carbohydrates: 21.01 g

Mushroom Chips

Preparation Time: 10 minutes

Cooking Time: 45-60 minutes

Servings: 2-4

Ingredients:

- 16 ounces of king oyster mushrooms
- 2 tablespoons ghee
- Kosher salt and ground pepper to taste

Directions:

1. Set the oven to 300F, then line two cookie sheets with parchment paper.
2. Cut every mushroom in half lengthwise, then cut with a mandolin into 1/8 inch slices or strips. Place them on cookie sheets with some room in between. Melt the ghee and brush it over the mushrooms, then season with the salt and pepper.
3. Bake for at least 45 minutes to 1 hour, until they are completely crisp. Store in airtight containers.

Nutrition: Calories: 62 kcal Protein: 5.58 g Fat: 2 g Carbohydrates: 7.97 g

Turmeric Gummies

Preparation Time: 5 minutes

Cooking Time: 4 hours and 10 minutes

Servings: 4

Ingredients:

- 6 tbsp. Maple syrup
- ½ cups Water
- 8 tbsp. Unflavored gelatin powder
- 1 tsp. Ground turmeric
- ¼ tsp. Ground pepper

Directions:

1. Mix the ground turmeric, maple syrup, and water in a pot set over medium heat. Stir constantly for 5 minutes before removing from heat and pouring in the gelatin powder. Stir with a wooden spoon to dissolve the gelatin.
2. Put back the pan on the heat and stir for another 2 minutes.
3. Turn off the heat and take the mixture to a deep bowl that you will seal with plastic wrap right after.
4. Refrigerate the mixture for about 4 hours.
5. It should be firm now, cut it into small squares, and serve or store.

Nutrition: Calories: 123 kcal Protein: 2.15 g Fat: 1.56 g Carbohydrates: 25.67 g

Mandarin Cottage Cheese

Preparation Time: 5 minutes

Cooking Time: 0 minutes

Servings: 1

Ingredients:

- 1/2 cup low-fat cottage cheese
- 1/2 cup canned mandarin mangos
- 1 1/2 tablespoons slivered almonds

Directions:

1. Place the cottage cheese in a bowl.
2. Drain the mandarin mangos, place them atop the cottage cheese, and sprinkle with almonds.

Nutrition: Calories: 360 kcal Protein: 26.24 g Fat: 21.37 g Carbohydrates: 15.22 g

Side dishes

Vegetable Rolls

Preparation Time: 30 minutes

Cooking Time: 0 minute

Servings: 8

Ingredients:

- Finely shredded red cabbage – ½ cup
- Grated carrot – ½ cup
- Julienne red bell pepper – ¼ cup
- Julienned scallion – ¼ cup, both green and white parts
- Chopped cilantro – ¼ cup
- Olive oil – 1 Tbsp.
- Ground cumin – ¼ tsp.
- Freshly ground black pepper – ¼ tsp.
- English cucumber – 1, sliced very thin strips

Directions:

1. In a bowl, toss together the black pepper, cumin, olive oil, cilantro, scallion, red pepper, carrot, and cabbage. Mix well.
2. Evenly divide the vegetable filling among the cucumber strips, placing the filling close to one end of the strip.
3. Roll up the cucumber strips around the filling and secure with a wooden pick.
4. Repeat with each cucumber strip.

Nutrition: Calories: 26 Fat: 2g Carb: 3g Phosphorus: 14mg Potassium: 95mg Sodium: 7mg Protein: 0g

Frittata With Penne

Preparation Time: 15 minutes

Cooking Time: 30 minutes

Servings: 4

Ingredients:

- Egg whites- 6
- Rice almond milk – ¼ cup
- Chopped fresh parsley – 1 Tbsp.
- Chopped fresh thyme – 1 tsp.
- Chopped fresh chives – 1 tsp.
- Ground black pepper
- Olive oil – 2 tsps.
- Small sweet onion – ¼, chopped
- Minced garlic – 1 tsp.
- Boiled and chopped red bell pepper – ½ cup
- Cooked penne – 2 cups

Directions:

1. Preheat the oven to 350F.
2. Whisk together the egg whites, rice almond milk, parsley, thyme, chives, and pepper.
3. Heat the oil in a skillet.
4. Sauté the onion, garlic, red pepper for 4 minutes or until they are softened.
5. Add the cooked penne to the skillet.

6. Transfer the egg mixture over the pasta and shake the pan to coat the pasta.
7. Leave the skillet on the heat for 1 minute to set the bottom of the frittata
8. Bake, the frittata for 25 minutes or until it is set and golden brown.
9. Serve.

Nutrition: Calories: 170 Fat: 3g Carb: 25g Phosphorus: 62mg Potassium: 144mg Sodium: 90mg Protein: 10g

Corn Bread

Preparation Time: 10 minutes

Cooking Time: 20 minutes

Servings: 10

Ingredients:

- Cooking spray for greasing the baking dish
- Yellow cornmeal – 1 ¼ cups
- All-purpose flour – ¾ cup
- Baking soda substitute – 1 tbsp.
- Granulated sugar – ½ cup
- Eggs – 2
- Unsweetened, unfortified rice almond milk – 1 cup
- Olive oil – 2 Tbsps.

Directions:

1. Preheat the oven to 425F.
2. Lightly spray an 8-by-8-inch baking dish with cooking spray. Set aside.
3. In a medium bowl, stir together the cornmeal, flour, baking soda substitute, and sugar.
4. In a small bowl, whisk together the eggs, rice almond milk, and olive oil until blended.
5. Place the wet ingredients to the dry ingredients and stir until well combined.
6. Pour the batter into the baking dish and bake for 20 minutes or until golden and cooked through.

7. Serve warm.

Nutrition: Calories: 198 Fat: 5g Carb: 34g Phosphorus: 88mg Potassium: 94mg Sodium: 25mg Protein: 4g

Tortilla Chips

Preparation Time: 15 minutes

Cooking Time: 10 minutes

Servings: 6

Ingredients:

- Granulated sugar – 2 tsps.
- Ground cinnamon – ½ tsp.
- Pinch ground nutmeg
- Flour tortillas – 3 (6-inch)
- Cooking spray

Directions:

1. Preheat the oven to 350F.
2. Line a baking sheet with parchment paper.
3. Mix the sugar, cinnamon, and nutmeg.
4. Lay the tortillas on a clean work surface and spray both sides of each lightly with cooking spray.
5. Sprinkle the cinnamon sugar evenly over both sides of each tortilla.
6. Cut the tortillas into 16 wedges each and place them on the baking sheet.
7. Bake the tortilla wedges, turning once, for about 10 minutes or until crisp.
8. Cool the chips serve.

Nutrition: Calories: 51 Fat: 1g Carb: 9g Phosphorus: 29mg Potassium: 24mg Sodium: 103 mg Protein: 1g

Soup & Stews

Easy Zucchini Soup

Preparation Time: 10 minutes

Cooking Time: 25 minutes

Servings: 4

Ingredients:

- 5 zucchinis, sliced
- 8 oz. cream cheese, softened
- 5 cups vegetable stock
- Pepper
- Salt

Directions:

1. Add zucchini and stock into the stockpot and bring to boil over high heat.
2. Turn heat to medium and simmer for 20 minutes.
3. Add cream cheese and stir until cheese is melted.
4. Puree soup using an immersion blender until smooth.
5. Season with pepper and salt.
6. Serve and enjoy.

Nutrition: Calories 245 Fat 20.3 g Carbohydrates 10.9 g Sugar 5.2 g Protein 7.7 g Cholesterol 62 mg Phosphorus: 110mg Potassium: 117mg Sodium: 75mg

Creamy Chicken Green Lettuce Soup

Preparation Time: 10 minutes

Cooking Time: 10 minutes

Servings: 6

Ingredients:

- 3 cups cooked chicken, shredded
- 1/8 tsp nutmeg
- 4 cup chicken broth
- 1/2 cup parmesan cheese, shredded
- 8 oz. cream cheese
- 1/4 cup butter
- 4 cup baby green lettuce, chopped
- 1 tsp garlic, minced
- Pepper
- Salt

Directions:

1. Melt butter in a saucepan over medium heat.
2. Add green lettuce and garlic and cook until green lettuce is wilted.
3. Add parmesan cheese and cream cheese and stir until cheese is melted.
4. Add remaining ingredients and stir everything well and cook for 5 minutes.

5. Season soup with pepper and salt.
6. Serve and enjoy.

Nutrition: Calories 361 Fat 25.6 g Carbohydrates 2.8 g Sugar 0.6 g Protein 29.5 g Cholesterol 121 mg Phosphorus: 110mg Potassium: 117mg Sodium: 75mg

Spicy Chicken Soup

Preparation Time: 10 minutes

Cooking Time: 5 minutes

Servings: 4

Ingredients:

- 2 cups cooked chicken, shredded
- 1/2 cup half and half
- 4 cups chicken broth
- 1/3 cup hot sauce
- 3 tbsp. butter
- 4 oz. cream cheese
- Pepper
- Salt

Directions:

1. Add half and half, broth, hot sauce, butter, and cream cheese into the blender and blend until smooth.
2. Pour blended mixture into the saucepan and cook over medium heat until just hot.
3. Add chicken stir well. Season soup with pepper and salt.
4. Serve and enjoy.

Nutrition: Calories 361 Fat 25.6 g Carbohydrates 3.3 g Sugar 1.1 g Protein 28.4 g Cholesterol 119 mg Phosphorus: 110mg Potassium: 117mg Sodium: 75mg

Tasty Pumpkin Soup

Preparation Time: 10 minutes

Cooking Time: 30 minutes

Servings: 6

Ingredients:

- 2 cups pumpkin puree
- 1 cup coconut cream
- 4 cups vegetable broth
- 1/2 tsp ground ginger
- 1 tsp curry powder
- 2 shallots, chopped
- 1/2 onion, chopped
- 4 tbsp. butter
- Pepper
- Salt

Directions:

1. Melt butter in a saucepan over medium heat.
2. Add shallots and onion and sauté until softened.
3. Add ginger and curry powder and stir well.
4. Add broth, pumpkin puree, and coconut cream and stir well. Simmer for 10 minutes.
5. Puree the soup using an immersion blender until smooth.
6. Season with pepper and salt.
7. Serve and enjoy.

Nutrition: Calories 229 Fat 18.4 g Carbohydrates 13 g Sugar 4.9 g Protein 5.6 g Cholesterol 20 mg Phosphorus: 120mg Potassium: 137mg Sodium: 95mg

Delicious Curried Chicken Soup

Preparation Time: 10 minutes

Cooking Time: 35 minutes

Servings: 10

Ingredients:

- 5 cups cooked chicken, chopped
- 1/4 cup fresh parsley, chopped
- 1/2 cup sour cream
- 1/4 cup apple cider
- 3 cups celery, chopped
- 1 1/2 tbsp. curry powder
- 10 cups chicken broth
- Pepper
- Salt

Directions:

1. Add all ingredients except sour cream and parsley into the stockpot and stir well.
2. Bring to boil over medium-high heat.
3. Turn heat to medium and simmer for 30 minutes.
4. Add parsley and sour cream and stir well.
5. Season with pepper and salt.
6. Serve and enjoy.

Nutrition: Calories 180 Fat 6.1 g Carbohydrates 3.7 g Sugar 1.9 g Protein 28.9 g Cholesterol 59 mg Phosphorus: 160mg Potassium: 107mg Sodium: 75mg

Dessert

Apple and Berries Ambrosia

Preparation time: 15 minutes

Cooking time: 0 minutes

Servings: 4

Ingredients:

- 2 cups unsweetened coconut milk, chilled
- 2 tablespoons raw honey
- 1 apple, peeled, cored, and chopped
- 2 cups fresh raspberries
- 2 cups fresh blueberries

Directions:

1. Spoon the chilled milk in a large bowl, then mix in the honey. Stir to mix well.
2. Then mix in the remaining ingredients. Stir to coat the fruits well and serve immediately.

Nutrition: calories: 386 fat: 21.1g protein: 4.2g carbs: 45.9g

Banana, Cranberry, and Oat Bars

Preparation time: 15 minutes

Cooking time: 40 minutes

Servings: 16 bars

Ingredients:

- 2 tablespoon extra-virgin olive oil
- 2 medium ripe bananas, mashed
- ½ cup almond butter
- ½ cup maple syrup
- 1/3 cup dried cranberries
- 1½ cups old-fashioned rolled oats
- ¼ cup oat flour
- ¼ cup ground flaxseed
- ¼ teaspoon ground cloves
- ½ cup shredded coconut
- ½ teaspoon ground cinnamon
- 1 teaspoon vanilla extract

Directions:

1. Preheat the oven to 400ºf (205ºc). Line an 8-inch square pan with parchment paper, then grease with olive oil.
2. Combine the mashed bananas, almond butter, and maple syrup in a bowl. Stir to mix well. Mix in the remaining ingredients and stir to mix well until thick and sticky.

3. Spread the mixture evenly on the square pan with a spatula, then bake in the preheated oven for 40 minutes or until a toothpick inserted in the center comes out clean.
4. Remove them from the oven and slice into 16 bars to serve.

Nutrition: calories: 145 fat: 7.2g protein: 3.1g carbs: 18.9g

Berry and Rhubarb Cobbler

Preparation time: 15 minutes

Cooking time: 35 minutes

Servings: 8

Ingredients:

- Cobbler:
- 1 cup fresh raspberries
- 2 cups fresh blueberries
- 1 cup sliced (½-inch) rhubarb pieces
- 1 tablespoon arrowroot powder
- ¼ cup unsweetened apple juice
- 2 tablespoons melted coconut oil
- ¼ cup raw honey
- Topping:
- 1 cup almond flour
- 1 tablespoon arrowroot powder
- ½ cup shredded coconut
- ¼ cup raw honey
- ½ cup coconut oil

Directions:

1. Preheat the oven to 350ºf (180ºc). Grease a baking dish with melted coconut oil. Combine the ingredients for the cobbler in a large bowl. Stir to mix well. Spread the mixture in the single layer on the baking dish. Set aside.

2. Combine the almond flour, arrowroot powder, and coconut in a bowl. Stir to mix well. Fold in the honey and coconut oil. Stir with a fork until the mixture crumbled.
3. Spread the topping over the cobbler, then bake in the preheated oven for 35 minutes or until frothy and golden brown. Serve immediately.

Nutrition: calories: 305 fat: 22.1g protein: 3.2g carbs: 29.8g

Citrus Cranberry and Quinoa Energy Bites

Preparation time: 15 minutes

Cooking time: 0 minutes

Servings: 12 bites

Ingredients:

- 2 tablespoons almond butter
- 2 tablespoons maple syrup
- ¾ cup cooked quinoa
- 1 tablespoon dried cranberries
- 1 tablespoon chia seeds
- ¼ cup ground almonds
- ¼ cup sesame seeds, toasted
- Zest of 1 orange
- ½ teaspoon vanilla extract

Directions:

1. Line a baking sheet with parchment paper. Combine the butter and maple syrup in a bowl. Stir to mix well.
2. Fold in the remaining ingredients and stir until the mixture holds together and smooth. Divide the mixture into 12 equal parts, then shape each part into a ball.
3. Arrange the balls on the baking sheet, then refrigerate for at least 15 minutes. Serve chilled.

Nutrition: calories: 110 fat: 10.8g protein: 3.1g carbs: 4.9g

Thank you!

Lightning Source UK Ltd.
Milton Keynes UK
UKHW050654280521
384527UK00007B/73